DRAWING
MANGA WOMEN

ANNA SOUTHGATE AND YISHAN LI

rosen publishing's
rosen
central®

NEW YORK

This edition published in 2013 by:

The Rosen Publishing Group, Inc.
29 East 21st Street
New York, NY 10010

Library of Congress Cataloging-in-Publication Data

Southgate, Anna.
Drawing manga women/Anna Southgate, Yishan Li.—First [edition].
    pages cm.—(Teen guide to drawing manga)
Includes bibliographical references and index.
ISBN 978-1-4488-9239-6 (library binding)—
ISBN 978-1-4488-9259-4 (pbk.)—
ISBN 978-1-4488-9260-0 (6-pack)
1. Women in art—Juvenile literature.
2. Girls in art—Juvenile literature.
3. Comic books, strips, etc.—Japan—Technique—Juvenile literature.
4. Cartooning—Technique—Juvenile literature. I. Li, Yishan. II. Title.
NC1764.8.W65S68 2013
741.5'1—dc23

2012034783

Manufactured in the United States of America

CPSIA Compliance Information: Batch #W13YA: For further information, contact Rosen Publishing, New York, New York, at 1-800-237-9932.

CONTENTS

INTRODUCTION

Maybe you are already a huge manga fan, with the ability to rattle off little-known facts about Sailor Moon at a moment's notice. Or perhaps this is your first foray into the Japanese art style known as manga. Maybe you just really love to draw and are looking for a great new style. Whatever your story is, if you want to learn more about drawing your own manga, this is the book for you.

The women and girls of manga art can be fun and flirty with big eyes and sassy dresses. Or they can be tough and fierce, heading into battle or hitting the ski slopes. The first thing you must ask yourself as you prepare to create your own female manga character is, "What kind of character do I want to create?"

What is her age? What is her style? Will she have short hair or long? With she be a traditional blond or dye her hair a quirky bright pink? It's all up to you, the artist. But where do you start?

In this book, you will learn all about giving your female manga characters their own great style, starting with the proper art tools. You'll learn how to age a character with a few pen strokes and what sets female characters apart from males. You'll learn how to draw your character from top to bottom, from faces and hair to bodies and clothing. Your character's style is all up to you.

Now, who do you want to create?

Chapter One
Manga Materials and Manga Tools

There are several ways to produce manga art. You can draw and colour images by hand, generate them on a computer or work using a combination of both. Whichever style suits you, there are plenty of options when it comes to buying materials. This section of the book outlines the basics in terms of paper, pencils, inking pens, markers and paints, and will help you to make choices that work for you.

MANGA MATERIALS AND MANGA TOOLS

Artists have their preferences when it comes to equipment, but regardless of personal favourites, you will need a basic set of materials that will enable you to sketch, ink and colour your manga art. The items discussed here are only a guide – don't be afraid to experiment to find out what works best for you.

PAPERS

You will need two types of paper – one for creating sketches, the other for producing finished colour artwork.

For quickly jotting down ideas, almost any piece of scrap paper will do. For more developed sketching, though, use tracing paper. Tracing paper provides a smooth surface, helping you to sketch freely. It is also forgiving – any mistakes can easily be erased several times over. Typically, tracing paper comes in pads. Choose a pad that is around 90gsm (24lb) in weight for best results – lighter tracing papers may buckle and heavier ones are not suitable for sketching. Once you have finished sketching out ideas, you will need to transfer them to the paper you want to produce your finished coloured art on. To do this, you will have to trace over your pencil sketch, so the paper you choose cannot be too opaque or heavy – otherwise you will not be able to see the sketch underneath. Choose a paper around 60gsm (16lb) for this. The type of paper you use is also important. If you are going to colour using marker pens, use marker or layout paper. Both of these types are very good at holding the ink found in markers. Other papers of the same weight can cause the marker ink to bleed, that is, the ink soaks beyond the inked lines of your drawing and produces fuzzy edges. This does not look good. You may wish to colour your art using other materials, such as coloured pencils or watercolours. Drawing paper is good for graphite pencil and inked-only art (such as that found in the majority of manga comic books),

Experiment with different papers to find the one that suits your style of drawing and colouring best. Watercolour papers can be ideal if you like using lots of wet colour like inks to render your manga.

while heavyweight watercolour papers hold wet paint and coloured inks and come in a variety of surface textures.

Again, don't be afraid to experiment: you can buy many types of papers in single sheets while you find the ones that suit your artwork best.

PENCILS

The next step is to choose some pencils for your sketches. Pencil sketching is probably the most important stage, and always comes first when producing manga art (you cannot skip ahead to the inking stage), so make sure you choose pencils that feel good in your hand and allow you to express your ideas freely.

Pencils are manufactured in a range of hard and soft leads. Hard leads are designated by the letter H and soft leads by the letter B. Both come in six levels – 6H is the hardest lead and 6B is the softest. In the middle is HB, a halfway mark between the two ranges. Generally, an HB and a 2B lead will serve most sketching purposes, with the softer lead being especially useful for loose, idea sketches, and the harder for more final lines.

Alternatively, you can opt for mechanical pencils. Also called self-propelling pencils, these come in a variety of lead grades and widths and never lose their point, making sharpening traditional wood-cased pencils a thing of the past. Whether you use one is entirely up to you

Graphite pencils are ideal for getting your ideas down on paper, and producing your initial drawing. The pencil drawing is probably the most important stage in creating your artwork. Choose an HB and a 2B to start with.

– it is possible to get excellent results whichever model you choose.

COLOURED PENCILS

Coloured pencils are effective and versatile colouring tools. A good box of pencils contains around 100 colours and will last for a long time, since a blunt pencil just needs sharpening, not replacing or refilling. Unlike with markers, successive layers of tone and shade can be built up with the same pencil, by gradually increasing the pressure on the pencil lead.

COPIC MARKERS
WARM AND COOL GREYS

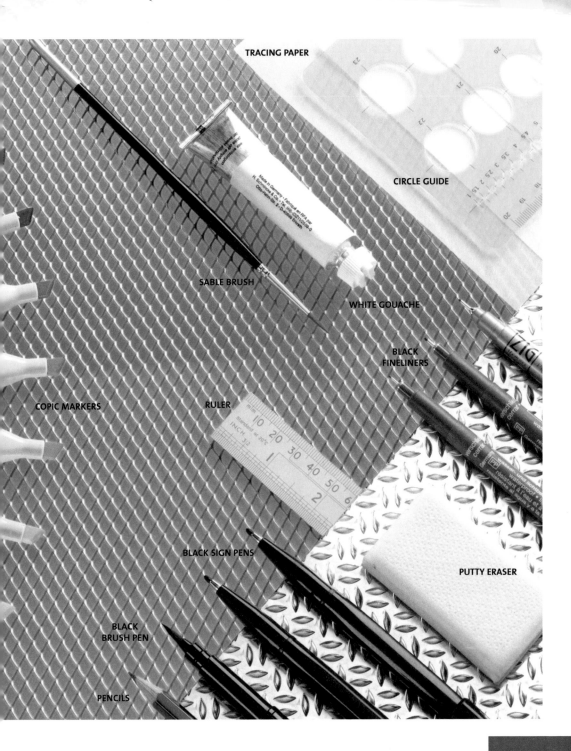

TRACING PAPER

CIRCLE GUIDE

SABLE BRUSH

WHITE GOUACHE

BLACK FINELINERS

COPIC MARKERS

RULER

BLACK SIGN PENS

PUTTY ERASER

BLACK BRUSH PEN

PENCILS

A good quality eraser or putty eraser is an essential item for removing unwanted pencil lines and for cleaning up your inked drawing before you start applying the colour.

Felt-tip pens are the ideal way to ink your sketches. A fineliner, medium-tip pen and sign pen should meet all of your needs, whatever your style and preferred subjects. A few coloured felt-tip pens can be a good addition to your kit, allowing you to introduce colour at the inking stage.

You can then build further colour by using a different colour pencil. Coloured pencils are also useful for adding detail, which is usually achieved by inking. This means that a more subtle level of detail can be achieved without having to ink in all lines. It is worth buying quality pencils. They do make a difference to the standard of your art and will not fade with age.

SHARPENERS AND ERASERS

If you use wooden pencils, you will need to get a quality sharpener; this is a small but essential piece of equipment. Electric sharpeners work very well and are also very fast; they last a long time too. Otherwise, a handheld sharpener is fine. One that comes with a couple of spare blades can be a worthwhile investment, to ensure that your pencils are always sharp. Along with a sharpener, you will need an eraser

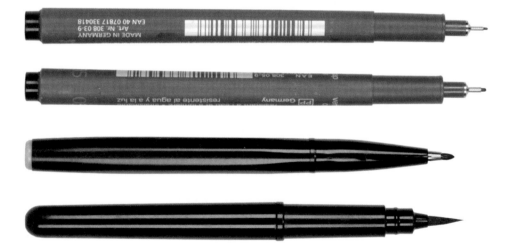

for removing any visible pencil lines from your inked sketches prior to colouring. Choose a high-quality eraser that does not smudge the pencil lead, scuff the paper, or leave dirty fragments all over your work. A soft putty eraser works best, since it absorbs pencil lead rather than just rubbing it away. For this reason, putty erasers do become dirty with use. Keep yours clean by trimming it carefully with scissors every now and then.

INKING PENS

The range of inking pens can be bewildering, but some basic rules will help you select the pens you need. Inked lines in most types of manga tend to be quite bold so buy a thin-nibbed pen, about 0.5mm, and a medium-size nib, about 0.8mm. Make sure that the ink in the pens is waterproof; this won't smudge or run. Next, you will need a medium-tip felt pen. Although you won't need to use this pen very often to ink the outlines of your characters, it is still useful for filling in small detailed areas of solid black. A Pentel pen does this job well. Last, consider a pen that can create different line widths according to the amount of pressure you put on the tip. These pens replicate brushes and allow you to create flowing lines such as those seen on hair and clothing. The Pentel brush pen does this very well, delivering a steady supply of ink to the tip from a replaceable cartridge. It is a good idea to test-drive a few pens at your art shop to see which ones suit you best. All pens should produce clean, sharp lines with a deep black pigment.

Markers come in a wide variety of colours, which allows you to achieve subtle variations in tone. In addition to a thick nib for broad areas of colour, the Copic markers shown here feature a thin nib for fine detail.

A selection of warm and cool greys is a useful addition to your marker colours and most ranges feature several different shades. These are ideal for shading on faces, hair, and clothes.

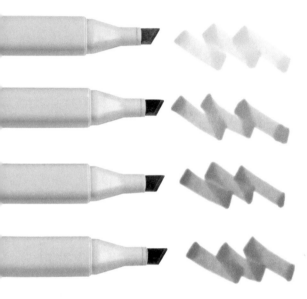

MARKERS AND COLOURING AIDS

Many artists use markers, rather than paint, to colour their artwork, because markers are easy to use and come in a huge variety of colours and shades. Good-quality markers, such as those made by Chartpak, Letraset or Copic, produce excellent, vibrant results, allowing you to build up multiple layers of colour so you can create rich, detailed work and precise areas of shading. Make sure that you use your markers with marker or layout paper to avoid bleeding. Markers are often refillable, so they last a long time. The downside is that they are expensive,

so choose a limited number of colours to start with, and add as your needs evolve. As always, test out a few markers in your art store before buying any.

However, markers are not the only colouring media. Paints and gouache also produce excellent results, and can give your work a distinctive look. Add white gouache, which comes in a tube, to your work to create highlights and sparkles of light. Apply it in small quantities with a good-quality watercolour brush. It is also possible to colour your artwork on computer. This is quick to do, although obviously there is a high initial outlay. It also tends to produce flatter colour than markers or paints.

DRAWING AIDS

Most of your sketching will be done freehand, but there are situations, especially with man-made objects such as the edges of buildings or the wheels of a car, when your line work needs to be crisp and sharp to create the right look.

If you are colouring with gouache or watercolour paint, then a selection of sizes of good quality sable watercolour brushes are invaluable.

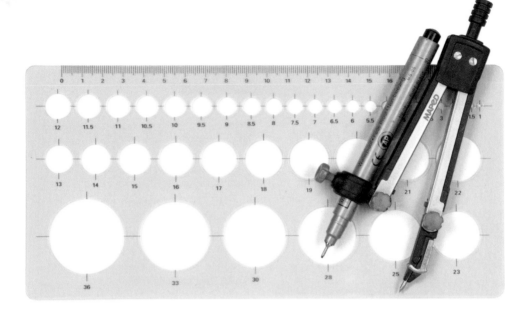

Rulers, circle guides and compasses all provide this accuracy. Rulers are either metal or plastic; in most cases, plastic ones work best, though metal ones tend to last longer. For circles, use a circle guide, which is a plastic sheet with a wide variety of different-sized holes stamped out of it. If the circle you want to draw is too big for the circle guide, use a compass that can hold a pencil and inking pen.

If you want to draw manga comic strips, a pencil and a standard 30cm (12in) ruler are the only tools you will need to plan out your panels. (It is also possible to draw them digitally on computer.) Just remember to buy a quality ruler with an edge that will suit your pencils and pens and won't chip over time. A plastic one will generally last longer than a wooden one. Creating speech bubbles inside the panels is best done by hand, but templates are available if you need help. They do make your work look neat, they are generally cheap to buy, and they

Working freehand allows great freedom of expression and is ideal when you are working out a sketch, but you will find times when precision is necessary. Use compasses or a circle guide for circles and ellipses to keep your work sharp. Choose compasses that can be adjusted to hold both pencils and pens.

do not need replacing often. You can buy them in most art shops. It is possible to order authentic manga templates from Japan, but these are not really necessary unless you want to start collecting authentic manga art equipment. You can make your own templates out of cardboard if the ones in the shops do not suit your needs.

DRAWING BOARD
A drawing board is useful, since working on a flat table for a long time can give you a backache. Lots of different models are available, but all should be adjustable to the angle at

which you want to work. They also come in a wide variety of sizes, from ones that sit on your lap or a tabletop to large work tables. If you do not want to invest in one immediately, it is possible to prop a piece of smooth, flat plywood about 60cm (24in) x 45cm (18in) on your desk. Put a small box underneath to create an angled surface.

A mannequin can be placed in different poses, helping you to visualise action and movement.

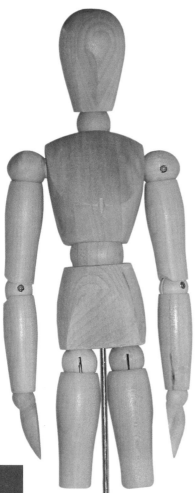

mannequin

A mannequin is an excellent tool for helping you to establish correct anatomical proportions, particularly for simpler poses such as walking and running. All the limbs are jointed to mimic human movement. They are also relatively cheap, but bear in mind that other reference materials may be necessary for more complicated movements, such as those involving martial arts. Photographic reference is often useful too.

USING A COMPUTER

When your sketches start coming easily and the more difficult features, such as texture and perspective, begin to look more convincing, you will be confident enough to expand on the range of scenes you draw. You might even begin to compose cartoon strips of your own or, at the very least, draw compositions in which several characters interact with each other – such as a battle scene.

Once you reach this stage, you might find it useful to start using a computer alongside your regular art materials. Used with a software program, like Adobe Photoshop, you can colour scanned-in sketches quickly and easily. You will also have a much wider range of colours to use, and can experiment at will. Moving one step further, a computer can save you a lot of time and energy when it comes to producing comic strips. Most software programs enable you to build a picture in layers. This means that you could have a general background layer – say a mountainous landscape – that always stays the same, plus a number of subsequent layers on

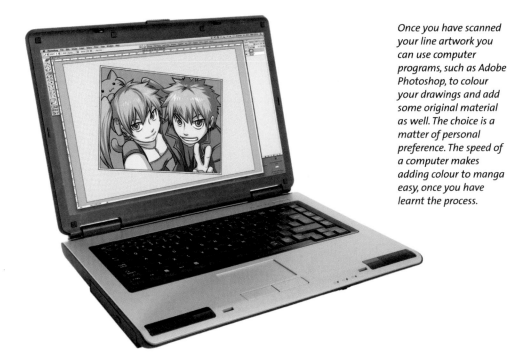

Once you have scanned your line artwork you can use computer programs, such as Adobe Photoshop, to colour your drawings and add some original material as well. The choice is a matter of personal preference. The speed of a computer makes adding colour to manga easy, once you have learnt the process.

which you can build your story. For example, you could use one layer for activity that takes place in the sky and another layer for activity that takes place on the ground. This means that you can create numerous frames simply by making changes to one layer, while leaving the others as they are. There is still a lot of work involved, but working this way does save you from having to draw the entire frame from scratch each time.

Of course, following this path means that you must invest in a computer if you don't already have one. You will also need a scanner and the relevant software. All of this can be expensive and it is worth getting your hand-drawn sketches up to a fairly accomplished level before investing too much money.

You can input a drawing straight into a computer program by using a graphics tablet and pen. The tablet plugs into your computer, much like a keyboard or mouse.

Chapter Two
Female Faces and Heads

A person's face says a great deal about their personality and this is an important factor when drawing animated figures. In manga art, there are plenty of opportunities for creating characters with different attitudes and expressions. This chapter shows how to draw a basic head shape from various angles, and the many ways in which you can add facial features to capture gender, mood and personality.

FACES AND AGE

All faces begin with the same very basic oval shape, divided vertically and horizontally into four sections. These guides make it easier to position the facial features. You can adapt the shape of the basic oval depending on the age and gender of your character.

Manga characters are usually quite androgynous. This girl has slightly larger eyes than a boy manga character and thinner eyebrows.

The adult female has softer features than the male. The face is more rounded at the chin, and the cheeks slightly fuller.

The face of the older manga woman is fuller than that of the man. Her nose is slimmer and she still has a good head of hair.

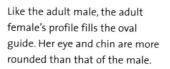

This girl has neat features with sparse detail. Her face is slightly more rounded, the eye a little bigger than a male character's.

Like the adult male, the adult female's profile fills the oval guide. Her eye and chin are more rounded than that of the male.

The older manga woman has a plumper, more rounded face than the man. Her neck is thicker and her cheeks fuller.

THREE-QUARTER VIEW

Drawing a face from the three-quarter view also works using an oval guideline, but this time it is slightly tilted. The important thing here is to draw the vertical guide (with a slight curve at the forehead) one-third of the way across the face. This will help to get the perspective right.

The girl's eyes are round. She has a very simple nose and mouth. Shading helps to make them realistic.

As with the full-face view, the young woman's jaw line is soft and smooth.

Note how the fuller face of the older woman spills out beyond the oval guide. This profile face is squarer than the others.

GIRL'S FACE FRONT VIEW

Here are the basic steps for drawing a young girl's face, face on. The same process can be used for any manga character, but remember to adapt the shape of the face and change the facial features depending on the kind of character you are creating.

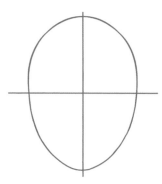 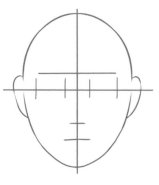 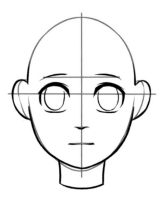

Draw your oval and divide it equally vertically (for symmetry) and horizontally (to provide a guide for positioning the eyes).

Now divide the oval into thirds horizontally. All facial features lie in the bottom two-thirds. Divide the face vertically by five.

Draw in facial features. The eyes dominate here. The eyebrows sit on the top-third horizontal guide, the nose on the second.

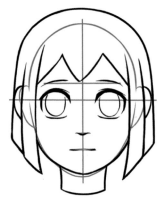  

Draw a rough outline for the girl's hair. It should stand proud of your oval guide, to give an impression of volume.

Draw in the finer details – pupils in the eyes, individual strands of hair. Go over your basic outline in ink. Erase any unwanted pencil.

Use typical manga colours to finish. Work in flat colour first and then add lighter or darker tones and highlights.

GIRL'S FACE *THREE-QUARTER VIEW*

A young girl seen from the three-quarter view. You can use the same steps for drawing a face looking in the opposite direction, but it is essential that you remember to move the position of the vertical guideline, as this is the key to getting the perspective right.

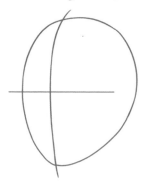 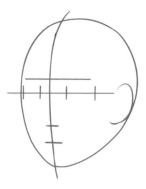 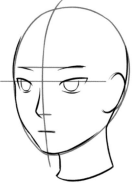

Draw a tapered oval with the usual horizontal guide. Then draw the vertical guide one-third in from the far side of the face.

Divide the face into equal thirds horizontally. Divide the face into fifths vertically, allowing for perspective.

Give more shape to the face and draw in the features. The nose should be in partial profile, the ear should rest on the oval guide.

Draw in an outline for the hair. Make it stand proud of the oval guide to give the impression of volume. Add detail to the ear.

Go over your drawing in ink, adding more detail to the eyes and giving more texture to the hair in places. Keep it simple.

Colour your work, using flat colours. Pay close attention to the direction of the light. Add lighter tones and highlights.

WOMAN'S FACE *LOOKING DOWN*

This woman is looking down and is viewed from a three-quarter view. Like the example on page 22, you can make her face the other way, but be sure to change the position of the vertical guide . The horizontal guide needs a downward curve to help with the positions of the eyes.

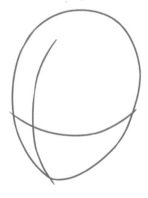

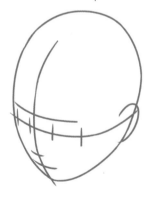

Draw a basic oval, tapered and tilted slightly to one side. Draw in the vertical and horizontal guides as described above.

Divide the face into thirds horizontally and fifths vertically. Note that the top third is bigger than the remaining two.

Position the facial features. The perspective here means that the ears are higher than the eyes and not level with them.

23

Draw in an outline for the hair. Notice how the hairline hugs the oval guide, because of the downward-looking perspective.

Go over your drawing in ink, adding more detail to the eyes. Give more texture to the hair and draw in a parting.

Colour your work using flat colour. Pay close attention to the direction of the light when it comes to the shaded areas.

EYE STYLES

The eyes are almost always the most important facial feature in manga art. Very often they are exaggerated in size and shape and dominate the face. You can use size, shape and colour to great effect when building on the personality of a character.

Children: Eyes are at their biggest in manga children, almost as tall as they are wide and with huge pupils. Boys' eyes (left) are more angular than girls' (right).

Teenagers: Although smaller than those of children, teenage eyes are still exaggerated. They retain distinctly angular (boys) and rounded (girls) forms.

Young adult: Mature manga characters tend to have more realistic eyes. The differences between male (left) and female (right) are less pronounced.

Older adult: There is more shaping to the eye socket in the older manga and a change in eyebrow colour. Notice how much smaller the pupils are.

DRAWING EYES

These are the two sorts of eye you are likely to use most – the larger-than-life youth's eye and the half-realistic adult eye. You can use these models to draw eyes for all your female characters. Just remember that female eyes are more rounded than male eyes.

BIG FEMALE EYES

Start with a partial outline. The eye is almost as tall as it is wide and has a large oval iris, part-obscured by the thick upper lid.

Draw minimal lines for the upper lid and eye socket. For female characters, draw out the outer corner to suggest lashes.

Go over your work in ink and colour the image. Use a striking shade for the iris and add bright highlights to give it more depth.

NOSE STYLES

There are several different styles to choose from when it comes to giving your manga character a nose. They range from a single line to mark the bottom of the nose, to the full-blown, human-style variety. You need to consider perspective carefully.

Drawing just the curve at the bottom of the nose is a simple option. Adding nostrils (left) is also an option. These are typically used for children.

Teenage noses tend to have a more angular quality, drawn using very simple lines (right). Casting a shadow to one side (left) helps define the shape.

Adult noses are more realistic in appearance. The shapes are drawn more fully. These types of nose work better when drawn with nostrils.

The noses of older manga characters are the most realistic of all. They can be smooth (left) or bony and gnarled (right).

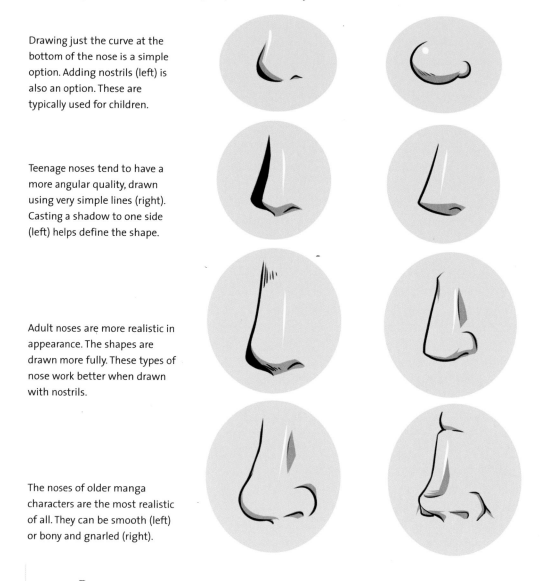

MOUTH STYLES

Manga mouths are often little more than a line drawn below the nose, but there are a number of alternatives to this. Once you start to draw different scenarios for your manga characters, you will also want to draw on a range of different expressions.

Female mouth, lips parted and visible teeth. The basic outline relies on colour for shape.

A simple open mouth, shouting or gasping maybe. The outline is basic and there are no lips.

Fuller female lips. The outline is strong and almost complete for a more realistic effect.

Seen from the side, this mouth reveals a vicious snarl. The lips are barely visible.

A human-looking female mouth. The outline is complete and gives shape to the full lips.

A laughing mouth, wide open with all the teeth visible. There is no need for lips.

EAR STYLES

When it comes to drawing ears, there are variations for a range of ages and scope for adapting them to suit any character you like. Of all the facial features in manga art, the ears tend to look the most realistic and you need to be able to draw them from a variety of different angles.

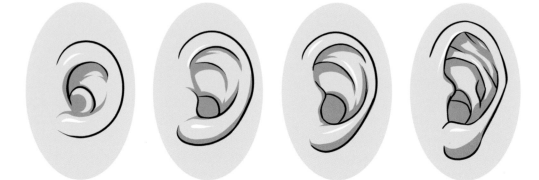

left to right The simplest style of ear is that of the chibi – the youngest character. The ear is almost round and has very little detail. In older children the ear is still simple, though longer. Young adults have more realistic ears, elongated in shape and with more detail. For the older manga characters a wholly realistic ear works well. This tends to have more shape and detail.

EARS AND ANGLES

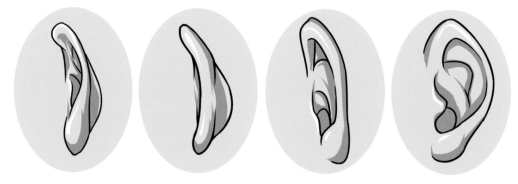

left to right Capturing the appearance of an ear accurately can be very difficult. They are awkward shapes and complex to draw from certain angles. You need to take perspective into account, which often involves foreshortening. These examples show the ear drawn variously from behind, a three-quarter view and side on. Notice how shape and visibility change.

SHORT HAIR BASICS

Many of your females characters will have short hair. The key to getting the look right is to follow the basic shape of your oval guide. Drawing a dotted hairline across the skull will help to get a realistic fringe and a more three-dimensional appearance.

left Short hair on girls can be both masculine and feminine. The bob is a classic girl's cut, and can be drawn either with a fringe or all one length and tucked behind the ears.

right Spiky hair on girls can be drawn longer than on boys. This gives it a softer, more feminine look. See how the colouring helps to create the texture.

FEMALE SHORT HAIR

When drawing short hair on a female character, it is sometimes important to keep it looking feminine. The example below shows a tight-cropped hairstyle where a slight curl helps to achieve a softer look. The colouring also helps.

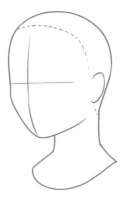

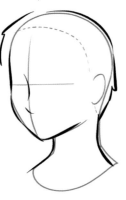

Draw your basic oval shape, with three-quarter view guidelines. Mark the hairline across the top of the head with a dotted line.

Work on the shape of the profile to soften the girl's features. Draw the outline of the hair, keeping it close to the back of the head.

Mark in some basic facial features and a couple of lines to capture the sweep of the fringe across the forehead.

Now work on the hair in greater detail. Little tufts here and there really soften the look. Use short, loose lines to draw them.

Make some of the tufts longer than others – at the sides, where they frame the girl's face. Use ink to finalise your drawing.

Colour your work. Use subtle dark tones along the fringe and towards the rear of the head. Add minimal highlights.

DRAWING MEDIUM-LENGTH HAIR

Medium-length hair tends to be about chin length. It can be straight or wavy. As for short hair, it help
to have the same guidelines that you use for drawing faces as well as a dotted guide for the hairline.

A girl with a chin-length bob. The simplicity of the cut is enhanced by the striking hair colour and the uneven fringe.

A girl with a waif-like look. Framing her face, the style has been achieved through subtle layering. The soft look is enhanced by the muted colour.

SHORT SCHOOLGIRL HAIR

This is a typical bob cut, with the hair the same length at the sides and rear of the girl's head and a long fringe. The hair is straight and thick. It is the volume of the hair that gives it a softer appearance. The hair has a glossy sheen, apparent in the lighter tones.

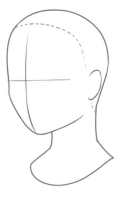

Draw your basic oval shape, with three-quarter view guidelines. Mark the hairline across the top of the head with a dotted line.

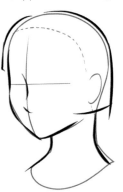

Draw a basic outline of the girl's profile and add a smooth line for the hair. See how it follows the oval guide quite closely.

This girl has a long fringe, drawn simply as a straight line across her forehead. Mark in some basic facial features.

Work some detail into the fringe, to show that it is made of many individual strands of hair. Draw the eyes in greater detail.

Draw any final details – giving the lips more definition, for example. Go over your artwork in ink and erase any pencil lines.

Colour your image, considering the direction of light. Be sparing with the darker tones, so that the glossy nature of the hair shows.

GIRL'S MESSY HAIR

Quite often, a hairstyle can give a character greater interest or more personality. Here, this backswept unruly style, gives the girl a certain air of mystery. Her angled eyes are more masculine than feminine, which adds to the interest.

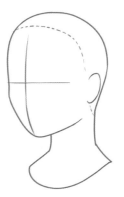

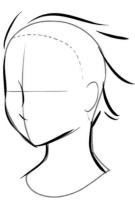

Draw your basic oval shape, with three-quarter view guidelines. Mark the hairline across the top of the head with a dotted line.

Add a basic outline of the girl's profile and add sweeping lines to suggest the hair. Keep them loose and free-flowing.

Position facial features, making the eyes more angular. Work on the hair. Note how it is swept back, away from the face.

Continue to work on the hair, keeping it loose and windswept. Draw a few strands tucked behind the ear at the side.

Finish the eyes and ear and give more shape to the neck. Go over your outline in ink, and erase unwanted pencil lines.

Colour your artwork, using flat colour before adding darker tones for shaded areas. There are no bright highlights to add.

DRAWING LONG HAIR

Long hair can mean anything from shoulder length. There is more scope here for a wider range of styles. Not only can you get to work on more intricate curls and colouring, but there are also plenty of opportunities for pony- and pigtails and all manner of accessories.

left Long hair is most often drawn on girls. Here the style is simple and straight. There is subtle layering where the hair frames the face.

right This is a more masculine look and could be used for boys as well as girls. The hair is thick and spiky, cropped short at the hairline and pushed to the back.

left This adaptation of the bob cut creates a harsh appearance. The lines are straight, rigid and angular. There is a certain coldness here, emphasised by the choice of hair colour.

right The softest look of the four, this hairstyle is very feminine. The tresses hang freely at the sides and rear, while the fringe falls into a natural parting.

33

GIRL'S LONG HAIR

This girl's long hairstyle gives her a very natural look. Swept back from the forehead, the hair is clipped at the sides and hangs freely at the back. The way that the hair sits on the girl's shoulders gives the impression that it is longer at the back than we can see.

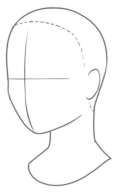

Draw your basic oval shape, with three-quarter view guidelines. Mark the hairline across the top of the head with a dotted line.

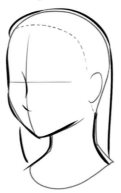

Add in a basic outline of the girl's profile and her hair. This style follows the oval guide closely across the top of the head.

Position the girl's facial features and draw the hair framing her face. It sits on the hairline guide and hangs loose at the sides.

Give shape to the hair, separating the tresses as they drape over the girl's shoulders. Draw her eyes in greater detail.

Finish the facial features and draw in the clips that stop the girl's hair from falling into her face. Go over your outline in ink.

Colour your artwork, using flat colour to start with. Most of the shading is to the rear. Add a few subtle highlights.

GIRL'S LONG MESSY HAIR

This is an unruly look that maintains a feminine air, largely thanks to the choice of colour. The shaggy tresses are achieved with bold, jagged lines whose curved elements help to keep the overall outline looking softer than it would if drawn using straight lines.

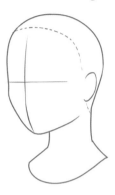

Draw your basic oval shape, with three-quarter view guidelines. Mark the hairline across the top of the head with a dotted line.

Work on the girl's profile and a basic outline of her hair. The shaggy look stands proud of the oval guide for more volume.

Position the girl's facial features and draw in the fringe. It flops over the forehead, framing the face at the sides.

Give shape to the hair, using bold sweeping lines to draw separate locks. Keep the lines short. Draw the eyes in greater detail.

Finish the facial features – the ear for example. Go over your outline in ink and erase any unwanted pencil lines.

Colour your artwork, using a soft flat colour. Work darker tones into the fringe and to the rear. Add a couple of highlights on top.

DRAWING HAIR FROM THE BACK

These characters are viewed from a three-quarter angle from the rear. This is achieved in the same way as the three-quarter angle (face on, see page 23). In this case, the hair, and not the facial features, take up two-thirds of the oval vertically and the face is seen in profile.

This short, spiky style is achieved by following the initial oval guide with a jagged outline. The rear of the head is in shadow.

Here the spiked hair is longer, which you can do by making your lines stand well proud of the oval guide.

This is an asymmetrical style, cropped tight across the head, while loose and long at the sides, back and fringe.

Note how the character's face is obscured in this three-quarter view. The hair is drawn thick and long all the way around.

This style shows how to draw soft gentle curls falling around the shoulders. Note how the crown of the head is prominent.

A high ponytail from the rear, showing how all of the hair is gathered up from the neck and away from the face.

GALLERY

You can use the principles on the previous pages to draw and colour any hairstyle you like. Use your imagination to create characters where the hair says as much about them as the clothes they are wearing. There really are no limits.

high ponytail

above Thick black hair tied back into a high ponytail and with a loose fringe swept from one side of the face to the other. There is no direct source of light, so there are no bright highlights.

futuristic

above Both the colour of the hair and the styling of it help to give this look a futuristic edge. It is close cropped with a short fringe and wing-like ponytails.

stepped bob

above This is a popular manga look, the shoulder-length hair set in two ridged tiers, topped by a deep straight-cut fringe.

girl next door

above More human-looking in terms of styling and colour, this shoulder-length hair is tied loosely at the back.

simple

above A simple style in a bold colour. The shading sees darker tones in the underside of the hair and deep within the fringe.

Chapter Four

Female Bodies

BODY COMPARISONS

Compare the male and female versions of the manga characters depicted on these pages. You will see straight away that the male versions tend to be a little taller than their female counterparts, yet there are a good number of similarities to take note of, too.

below
The elderly. In terms of proportion, older characters tend to divide into fifths. The head makes up one-fifth, the torso two-fifths and the legs two-fifths. The shapes of their bodies are not as well-defined as in younger characters, and they wear loose-fitting clothes.

above
The mature adult. Body proportions work on sevenths, here, where the head is one-seventh, the torso roughly two-and-a-half, and the legs roughly three-and-a-half. Figures are lean and muscled in men and more

above

Chibis. Physically, there are no differences between male and female chibis – this has to come down to hair and clothing. Proportionally, their heads make up one-third of their body size.

above

Teenagers. Differences between male and female characters begin to emerge as they enter their teenage years. Boys are a little taller and more muscular than girls, while girls are slimmer with natural curves and well-defined waistlines. Facial features in girls tend to be softer. Proportions are the same as for the mature adult.

right

Manga children. Boys and girls are almost identical and usually only distinguishable by their clothing and hairstyles. Boys tend to have less shapely limbs and thicker necks. Proportions are the same as for the elderly.

Teenage girl. Like the boy opposite, her proportions are exaggerated. She is tall and skinny, almost androgynous.

Adult female. Although the proportions are more human here, the woman still has an impossibly thin waist.

A full-bodied adult female. Her anatomy is realistic in terms of proportion, with a slightly exaggerated chest and waist.

DANCING GIRL

This is a wonderful balletic pose. The girl is bright and cheerful and light on her feet. You need to be able to capture the idea that the girl is in motion. This will give your finished picture a more fluid look. You can apply the steps to a range of dance poses.

Build on your structure. Draw each body part as a simple shape and use ovals or circles to link these shapes together at the joints.

Review your outline. You need to capture the tension in the outstretched arms and legs.

Start by drawing a basic structure in pencil. Note how the arms and legs are outstretched. Try to to capture the physical strength and flexibility in the pose.

Use your structural work to draw a solid outline. Try to maintain the girl's strength and flexibility. Draw in guides for the hair and facial features.

GIRL SQUATTING

This is a simple seated pose, half kneeling, half squatting on the floor. It can be used with any characters, male or female, young or old.

Use a pencil to sketch a basic structure. The upper body leans forward slightly, with the legs bent at the knees and tucked underneath.

Use simple geometric shapes to draw the body parts, linking them together at the joints with circles or ovals. Think about perspective.

Use this structure to draw a solid outline. Think about the girl's muscular make-up as you do this. Draw in the guides for hair and facial features.

Draw in the girl's eyes and an outline of her hair. Give more shape to her body, drawing her abdomen more accurately.

42

Still on the abdomen, add feint lines to mark her clothing. Give more shape to the legs and arms. Consider the perspective again.

Once you are happy with your pencil drawing, go over just the outline of the girl's body in ink. Take care to follow your sketch accurately.

Now draw the girl's clothes, using pencil. Her outfit is simple. You need only draw an outline, which you can then go over in ink.

Now you can add colour to your drawing. Use flat colour to start with. You can then build on the areas of light and shade.

GIRL BENDING

This is a very casual pose, with the girl bending down as if she has dropped something or is about to pick something up. As the one hand goes down towards the floor, the other rises up to counterbalance the action.

Use a pencil to draw your basic structure. Note the positions of the arms and that both legs are a little bent.

Use your basic structure to draw a solid outline. Make the girl more shapely, rounding her shoulders and hips. Draw in guides for hair and facial features.

Use a series of shapes for the body parts and link them together at the joints with circles or ovals. Think about body shape and perspective.

The bent knee should be slightly in front of the straighter leg. Refine the shapes of the hands and feet.

Chapter Five
Female Clothing

A character's clothing says a great deal about her personality. From a nurse's uniform to the ditsy striped stockings of your friendly waitress, there are all sorts of ways to make manga characters individual. This section of the book looks at drawing clothing of all styles and offers advice on how to draw the diverse range of materials from which they are made.

FINDING INSPIRATION

Once you start to develop your stories, you will want to draw manga characters of all kinds. Some will be based on modern-day people, while others might be inspired by times gone by. No doubt you will also have fun exploring your very own vision of the future.

A young female police officer in a blue uniform. It helps to think of accessories that might go with a character's job – the hat and whistle, for example.

Search through books or the internet for examples of traditional costumes from across the world. Japanese kimonos, Spanish flamenco dresses and Indian saris can all form the basis of a character's outfit.

Always think about the age of the character you are designing clothes for. The short skirt of this Japanese school uniform might not work on an older girl.

Think of the many careers that involve the wearing of a uniform from hotel staff, to firefighters and elaborate on them to make your own designs.

SEASONS AND MATERIALS

Before you start to draw an outfit, think carefully about what it is used for and what materials it should be made from. Consider seasonal variations, too, as these will have an impact on the design and weight of fabric.

left In the hotter months, shirts and dresses tend to have short sleeves or no sleeves at all. Typical fabrics include light cottons, silks and Lycra.

right The many styles of swimsuit fall into two general groups: bikini and all-in-one. They tend to be made from Lycra and have fun, colourful designs.

left Summer fabrics often cling to the natural curves of the body. Polyester tends to be stiffer than cotton or Lycra and so has sharp creases. Use thin inking lines to help capture the shape.

right Cotton and Lycra have soft creases that follow the natural shape of the body. You, also need to consider body shape when drawing in any shadows.

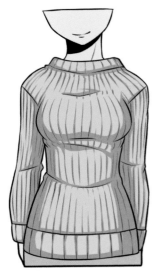

left Clothing for the colder months is usually made from thicker materials, such as wool and fur. They tend to have more interesting textures.

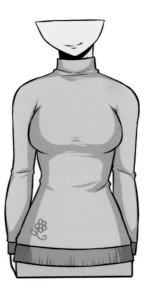

right Woollen garments tend to make the body look slightly fatter. Even though they follow the body shape, the natural curves are less well defined.

left Fur is a particular winter favourite and can be used to give clothing a soft trim around the hem- or neckline. It tends to have a single, massed shape.

right Owing to their thickness, winter clothes tend to have fewer folds or drapes. Creases, when they do occur, are often soft and deep.

COTTON T-SHIRT

A wardrobe staple, the simple cotton T-shirt can be long and baggy or close-fitting and tight. It is one of the simplest garments to draw and can be adapted in so many ways – with embellishments, logos, trim – and in many colours.

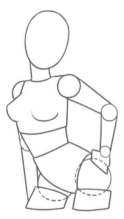

Draw a pencil outline of your figure, using a series of geometric shapes.

Use your pencil outline as a guide for drawing the T-shirt. Keep it loose at the sleeves and mid-rif. Draw facial guides.

Draw the hair and facial features. Give shape to the arms and legs. Draw feint lines to suggest creases in the cotton fabric.

Add trim to the collar and sleeves to finish. Go over your drawing in ink and erase any unwanted pencil lines.

Colour your artwork. Use your crease lines to place shadows, giving shape to the body beneath the T-shirt.

POLYESTER SHIRT

Polyester is a more rigid fabric than Lycra or cotton, and so clothes made from it tend to have a stiffer quality. This makes it ideal for shirts for both men and women.

Draw a pencil outline of your figure, using a series of geometric shapes.

Use your pencil outline as a guide for drawing the shirt. Use short, stiff lines to capture the crisp fabric. Draw facial guides.

Draw the hair and facial features. Shape the arms and legs. Add lines to suggest creases in the fabric or where it is stretched.

Go over your drawing in ink and erase any unwanted pencil lines. Add finishing touches, such as the front seam and sleeve trim.

Colour your work. Use the crease lines to place shadows, and keep the contrast high to reflect the stiffness of the fabric.

51

DENIM JEANS

A popular choice for male and female characters of all ages, denim jeans can be long or short, skinny or baggy. You could also use this example for drawing leggings.

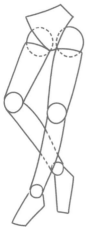

Draw a pencil outline of your figure, using a series of geometric shapes.

Use your pencil outline as a guide for drawing the jeans. These ones are skinny.

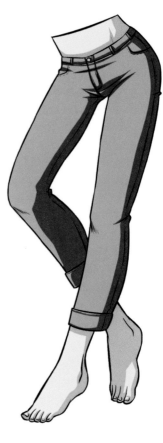

Start to add a few details – the zip, waistband and turnups, for example. Give shape to the feet.

Go over your drawing in ink, adding pockets and seams. Draw lines where the denim is creased.

Colour your image. Use flat colour to render the matt quality of the denim. Keep shadows soft.

FUR COAT

Another wool coat with fur trim. The design is such that the coat is well-fitted, so defining the bust and waist. The fabric is stiff, with minimal creasing.

Draw a pencil outline of your figure, using a series of geometric shapes.

Draw the outline of the coat, keeping it close to your guides. Draw in the facial guides.

Draw the hair and facial features. Give more shape to the coat, adding decorative details.

Go over your drawing in ink, adding final details, such as the buckles, and finish the fur.

Colour your work using soft, muted colours. Use shadows to give more shape to the body.

53

SUN VISOR

This is a very simple design – simply the peak of a baseball cap on a strap. You can adapt it to suit a wide range of characters from sun-seeker to dubious dude.

Use pencil to draw your basic oval shape, with three-quarter view guidelines. Draw in your character's facial features.

Sketch in an outline of the hair – in this case long and shaggy. Draw in the visor, making sure you get the perspective right.

Now draw in the headband. Note how it disappears beneath the hair towards the rear. Draw in the girl's neck and ear.

Add any final details – a few lines to define the crown of the head and shaping to the girl's neck. Go over your artwork in ink.

Colour your work using a subtle change in tone to emphasise the shaded areas. Note how the visor casts a shadow over the face.

WOOLLY SCARF

The scarf is a popular winter accessory and is usually made from a soft knit. There are various ways to wear them – tied loosely at the neck, wrapped around once or twice or simply draped around the shoulders.

Start by drawing a pencil outline of your figure using basic geometric shapes. Build on your outline to sketch the girl in more detail, adding hair and facial features.

Give more shape to the scarf, marking crease lines where it folds and drawing the individual tassels at the ends. Go over your work in ink.

Draw in the girl's clothes, adding an outline of the scarf. In this case it is wrapped around the neck with the ends hanging loose.

Colour your work. This scarf is a mid-blue. Use the creases as guides for adding some soft shadows in the folds.

METAL ARMOUR

Metal is a favourite for the more outlandish manga characters. Its shiny, rigid surfaces make it useful for all manner of wild designs.

Draw a pencil outline of your figure, using a series of geometric shapes.

Draw the outline of the armour, bearing in mind its rigidity. Draw in the facial guides.

Add hair and facial features. Work on the armour, adding joints for separate metal plates.

Go over your drawing in ink, adding any final decorative details to the design.

Colour your work. The metal has a soft sheen. Use subtle changes of tone to reflect this.

GALLERY

Being able to draw clothes accurately is key to creating realistic-looking manga characters. It is important to consider the weight and texture of the fabric and the body shape of the wearer. The way in which the fabric has been used or is being worn is also significant.

pleated skirt

above Gathered and pleated fabrics, as used for this skirt, have creases and folds at regular intervals.

Lycra vest

above All of the body's natural curves are clearly defined owing to the clingy, stretchy nature of this fabric.

leggings

above Lycra-based, leggings are naturally skin-tight, creasing only when joints are bent.

ruffled skirt

above Complex, multilayered or gathered clothing will have a large number of folds. They may not all go in the same direction.

gathered top

above Grasped areas of fabric have loose folds radiating from a tight pinched centre.

GIRL WEARING KIMONO

The kimono is a traditional form of dress in Japan, worn by both men and women. They are often made from exquisite fabrics with all manner of elaborate patterns.

Use your outline as a guide for drawing the kimono. Use simple lines in order to achieve the basic shape of the garment.

Finalise the outline of the kimono and go over your whole artwork using ink.

Draw a pencil outline using a series of geometric shapes. Give the woman a stance in keeping with the style of her clothing.

Give the character some hair and draw in the facial features. Begin to add detail to the kimono and draw the feet.

Consider where the lightweight fabric might be folded or creased, such down the front of the skirt area. Draw a few lines for emphasis here.

Colour your work. Pay particular attention to areas of light and shade, and use highlights to emphasise the folds.

Start to add detail. Draw in lines to show how the layers build up beneath the outer garment. Give more shape to the sash at the waist and draw in the shoes.

Add any final ink details, such as the pretty decorative elements in the fabric.

COURT DRESS

This character is wearing clothes based on those worn by early 19th-century European royalty or aristocracy. The lines are elegant and feminine, yet maintain a rigid formality. It always helps to source pictures for any period of dress style on which to base your own designs.

Use your outline as a guide for drawing the dress. Use simple lines to achieve the basic shape. The outfit is fitted above the waist and reaches the floor in terms of length.

Finalise your basic outline of the dress, drawing in the decorative border of the upper section.

Begin by drawing a pencil outline using simple geometric shapes. Give your character an elegant stance, in keeping with the style of her clothes.

Give your character some hair and draw in the facial features. Work a little more on the outline, drawing in the loose-fitting sleeves and shaped hemline.

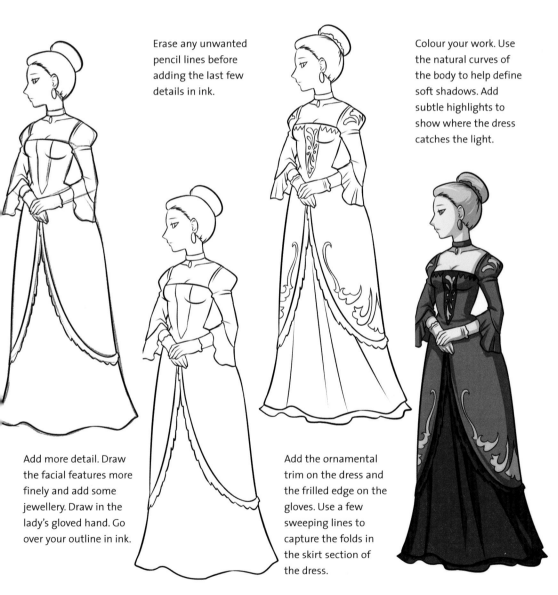

Erase any unwanted pencil lines before adding the last few details in ink.

Colour your work. Use the natural curves of the body to help define soft shadows. Add subtle highlights to show where the dress catches the light.

Add more detail. Draw the facial features more finely and add some jewellery. Draw in the lady's gloved hand. Go over your outline in ink.

Add the ornamental trim on the dress and the frilled edge on the gloves. Use a few sweeping lines to capture the folds in the skirt section of the dress.

JAPANESE SCHOOLGIRL

The traditional Japanese school uniform for girls is based on a sailor-suit design. There are many variations, but most of them feature a blue-and-white colour scheme.

Use your outline as a guide for drawing the uniform. Use simple lines to achieve the basic shape.

Once the outline is complete, you can go over your work in ink.

Begin by drawing a pencil outline using simple geometric shapes. Give your figure a schoolgirl pose.

Now draw the outline of the body, giving more shape to the natural curves. Give the character hair and draw in the facial features.

Erase your pencil lines in preparation for adding the finer ink details and colour.

Colour your work. Add very soft shadows in the folds of the shirt, and stronger ones in the pleats of the skirt. Add subtle highlights.

Draw in a crease to emphasise the loose, flowing nature of the sleeve. Give the skirt pleats. Add a sock line and draw the shoes.

Add final ink details, such as the short lines defining the bust area, extra creases in the sleeve and the stripe in the blue trim. Finish the shoes and socks.

BUSINESS WOMAN

Clothing for the office environment tends to be more formal than everyday or weekend wear. This outfit has a matching skirt and blouse in muted colours. The clothes are fitted, so giving the character a smarter appearance.

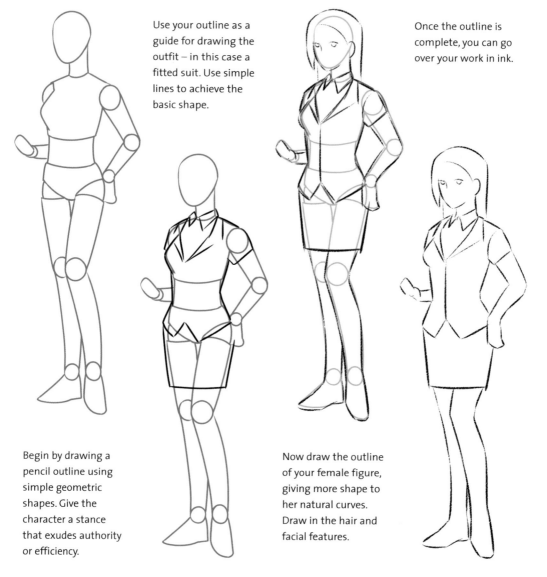

Use your outline as a guide for drawing the outfit – in this case a fitted suit. Use simple lines to achieve the basic shape.

Once the outline is complete, you can go over your work in ink.

Begin by drawing a pencil outline using simple geometric shapes. Give the character a stance that exudes authority or efficiency.

Now draw the outline of your female figure, giving more shape to her natural curves. Draw in the hair and facial features.

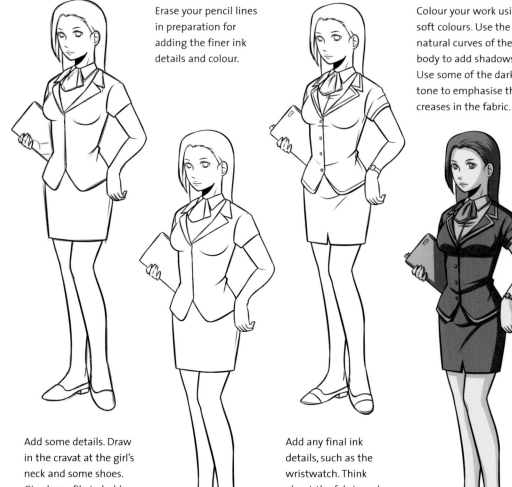

Erase your pencil lines in preparation for adding the finer ink details and colour.

Colour your work using soft colours. Use the natural curves of the body to add shadows. Use some of the darker tone to emphasise the creases in the fabric.

Add some details. Draw in the cravat at the girl's neck and some shoes. Give her a file to hold.

Add any final ink details, such as the wristwatch. Think about the fabric and mark some creases. Draw in the trim on the suit and some buttons.

65

CUTE GIRL

This character has a cute baby-doll look. She is clearly a teenager, but wears clothes and accessories associated with children. It is a popular look in manga art, but is only ever used for young female characters.

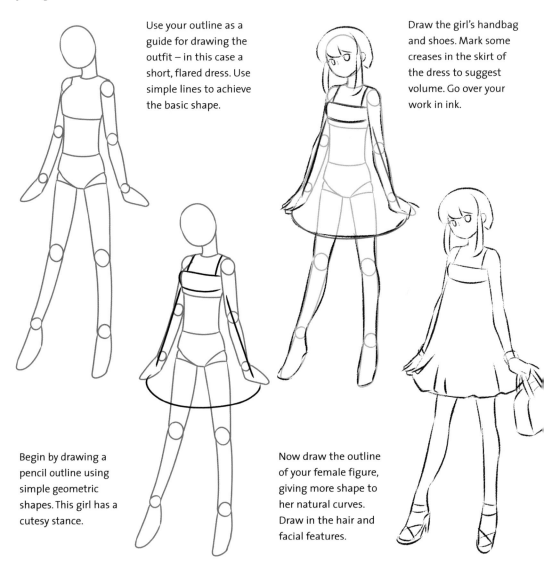

Use your outline as a guide for drawing the outfit – in this case a short, flared dress. Use simple lines to achieve the basic shape.

Draw the girl's handbag and shoes. Mark some creases in the skirt of the dress to suggest volume. Go over your work in ink.

Begin by drawing a pencil outline using simple geometric shapes. This girl has a cutesy stance.

Now draw the outline of your female figure, giving more shape to her natural curves. Draw in the hair and facial features.

Erase your pencil lines in preparation for adding the finer ink details and colour.

Colour your work using baby-doll colours. Use darker tones to emphasise the creases in the fabric. Drop in a few highlights.

Add more detail. Give the girl some jewellery, complete the straps on the dress and work on the handbag design. Finish the shoes.

Add any final ink details, such as the pretty trim on the dress and the pussy cat image on the bag.

PIRATE

This character has a great other-worldly quality. Dressed as a pirate, complete with cutlass, this is a genuine tom-boy and not just a case of dressing up. You could adapt the look for a Robin Hood type character with a bow and arrow.

Use your outline as a guide for drawing the outfit – in this case a jumpsuit. Use simple lines to achieve the basic shape.

Once the outline is complete, you can go over your work in ink.

Begin by drawing a pencil outline using simple geometric shapes. This girl has a defiant stance.

Now draw the girl's arms and ankles. Then draw her hair and facial features. Add outlines for the leather boots.

Erase your pencil lines in preparation for adding the finer ink details and colour.

Colour your work. Use the natural curves of the body to add shadows. Use some of the darker tone to emphasise the creases in the fabric.

Start to work on the detail. Draw the sash around the girls' waist and the cutlass by her side. Give more shape to the boots.

Add any final ink details, such as the lacing on the boots and jumpsuit and creases in the lightweight jumpsuit fabric. Finish the sash and headband.

NURSE

Nurse uniforms differ from country to country, so do a little research to find a design you like. Adapt this example to design uniforms for other characters, for example, a woman from a religious order or a schoolgirl.

Using your pencil guide, to sketch in the uniform. This example has a simple knee-length coat and hat.

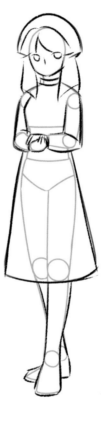

Once the outline is complete, you can go over your work in ink.

Begin by drawing a pencil outline using simple geometric shapes. This woman has a benign stance.

Now draw the outline of your female figure, giving more shape to her natural curves. Draw in the hair and facial features.

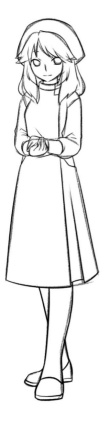

Erase your pencil lines in preparation for adding the finer ink details and colour.

Colour your work using soft colours. Use the natural curves of the body to add shadows. Use some of the darker tone to emphasise the creases in the fabric.

Work on the finer details now – the front seam of the coat and pleated detail. Give more shape to the sleeves and add shoes.

Add any final ink details, such as the decorative elements on the hat and shoes and the pocket on the coat.

schoolgirl

below This is an alternative version of the school uniform seen on pages 62–63. This is a slightly less formal example.

native American

above This outfit has a zigzag pattern inspired by native American costume.

crop top and shorts

above The streetwise look of a girl who knows her style. She wears a fitted crop top and shorts with chunky boots.

sloppy jumper

right The ditsy look of this sloppy jumper is echoed in the one up, one down stripy tights.

ancient world

left The simple lines and apron front of this outfit were inspired by clothing once worn in ancient Rome and Greece.

theatrical cat

above An outfit for a school play or a fancy-dress party, this girl is dressed in a huge cat costume. Note the texture of the fur.

country girl

above The simple dress of a little country girl, married with durable leather boots.

fancy dress

left A great-fun outfit for Halloween, this costume combines a host of motifs from the devil's horns and tail to batwings and a pumpkin.

girl next door

right This outfit has a thrown-together look to it, reminiscent of teenagers at the weekend.

GLOSSARY

androgynous   Having both male and female characteristics.

angular   Composed of many, often sharp-cornered, angles.

chibi   A small, cute manga child or animal.

compass   A technical drawing instrument used for drawing arcs and circles.

drawing board   A desk designed specifically for drawing.

graphics tablet   A computer device that uses a pen-like device to enable a user to hand-draw images.

kimono   A traditional Japanese robe with wide sleeves and an ankle-length hem.

Lycra   Also known as Spandex, an elastic synthetic fiber often used in sportswear.

manga   Art style based in Japanese comic art.

mechanical pencils   A pencil that contains a replaceable lead that can be extended as the point is worn down.

outline   A first basic pencil sketch that helps with basic proportion before art is completed.

shading   The process of darkening a piece of art in certain places in order to create the illusion of depth.

sketch   A fast freehand drawing.

tracing paper   Translucent paper that, when laid over the top of a picture, allows the picture to show through in order for it to be replicated.

FOR MORE INFORMATION

Animazing Gallery
54 Greene Street
New York, NY 10013
(212) 226-7374
Web site: http://www.animazing.com
This gallery exhibits a unique collection of original and
    limited-edition animation and illustration artwork that
    indulges the senses and emotions with color and
    playfulness.

Japan Society
333 East 47th Street
New York, NY 10017
(212) 832-1155
Web site: http://www.japansociety.org
Japan Society is an American nonprofit organization that
    brings the people of Japan and the United States closer
    together through mutual understanding, appreciation,
    and cooperation.

Midwest Comic Book Association
P.O. Box 131475
Saint Paul, MN 55113
(612) 237-1801
Web site: http://midwestcomicbook.com
This association organizes events where comic book enthusi-
    asts and collectors can get together and share and trade
    their finds.

Midtown Comics
200 West 40th Street
New York, NY 10018
Web site: http://www.midtowncomics.com
This comic book store has a huge selection of manga that
    can be ordered online.

Museum of Comic and Cartoon Art
594 Broadway, Suite 401
New York, NY 10012
Web site: http://moccany.org
This New York art gallery features a large collection of
    comic book art.

Web Sites

Due to the changing nature of Internet links, Rosen Publishing
has developed an online list of Web sites related to the subject
of this book. This site is updated regularly. Please use this link to
access the list:

http://www.rosenlinks.com/MAMA/Women

Amberlyn, J.C. *Drawing Manga Animals, Chibis, and Other Adorable Creatures.* New York, NY: Watson-Guptill, 2009.

Bunyapen, Supittha. *Shojo Wonder Manga Art School: Create Your Own Cool Characters and Costumes with Markers.* Cincinnati, OH: IMPACT, 2011.

Casaus, Fernando. *The Monster Book of Manga: Draw Like the Experts.* New York, NY: HarperCollins, 2006.

Crilley, Mark. *Mastering Manga with Mark Crilley.* Cincinnati, OH: IMPACT, 2012.

Flores, Irene. *Shojo Fashion Manga Art School: How to Draw Cool Looks and Characters.* Cincinnati, OH: IMPACT, 2009.

Hart, Christopher. *Basic Anatomy for the Manga Artist: Everything You Need to Start Drawing Authentic Manga Characters.* New York, NY: Watson-Guptill, 2011.

Hart, Christopher. *Manga for the Beginner: Everything You Need to Start Drawing Right Away!* New York, NY: Watson-Guptill, 2008.

Hart, Christopher. *Manga for the Beginner Chibis: Everything You Need to Start Drawing the Super-Cute Characters of Japanese Comics.* New York, NY: Watson-Guptill, 2010.

Hart, Christopher. *Manga Mania Magical Girls and Friends: How to Draw the Super-Popular Action Fantasy Characters of Manga.* New York, NY: Watson-Guptill, 2006.

Hills, Doug. *Manga Studio for Dummies.* Hoboken, NJ: Wiley, 2008.

The Monster Book of Manga: Girls. New York, NY: Harper Design, 2008.

The Monster Book of More Manga: Draw Like the Experts. New York, NY: Harper Design, 2007.

INDEX

H

hair, drawing, 29–37
  from the back, 36
  gallery, 37
  long hair, 33–34
  long messy hair, 35
  medium-length hair, 30
  messy hair, 32
  short hair, 29–30
  short hair basics, 29
  short schoolgirl hair, 31

I

inking pens, 13

M

mannequin, 16
markers and colouring aids, 14
materials and tools, to create
    manga, 7–17
mouth styles, 27

N

nose styles, 26

P

papers, 8–9
pencils, 9
  coloured, 9–12
pens, inking, 13

S

sharpeners, 12
squatting girl, drawing a, 42–43

W

woman's face looking down,
    drawing, 23–24

About the Authors

Anna Southgate is an experienced writer and editor who has worked extensively for publishers of adult illustrated reference books. Her recent work has included art instruction books and providing the text for a series of six manga titles.

Yishan Li is a professional manga artist living in Edinburgh, Scotland. Her work has been published in the UK, United States, France, and Switzerland. She has published many books on manga, and she also draws a monthly strip, *The Adventures of CGI, for CosmoGirl!*